T0065685

My Sophia

TONJA MCCLAIN

WESTBOW
PRESS®
A DIVISION OF THOMAS NELSON
& ZONDERVAN

This book is a work of non-fiction. Unless otherwise noted, the author and the publisher make no explicit guarantees as to the accuracy of the information contained in this book and in some cases, names of people and places have been altered to protect their privacy.

WestBow Press books may be ordered through booksellers or by contacting:

WestBow Press
A Division of Thomas Nelson & Zondervan
1663 Liberty Drive
Bloomington, IN 47403
www.westbowpress.com
844-714-3454

Because of the dynamic nature of the Internet, any web addresses or links contained in this book may have changed since publication and may no longer be valid. The views expressed in this work are solely those of the author and do not necessarily reflect the views of the publisher, and the publisher hereby disclaims any responsibility for them.

Any people depicted in stock imagery provided by Getty Images are models, and such images are being used for illustrative purposes only. Certain stock imagery © Getty Images.

Scripture taken from the King James Version of the Bible.

ISBN: 978-1-6642-7702-1 (sc)
ISBN: 978-1-6642-7703-8 (e)

Library of Congress Control Number: 2022916155

Print information available on the last page.

WestBow Press rev. date: 10/26/2022

My Sophia

Lady of wisdom
Who has never ceased in giving
To those in need
Be family, friend, or stranger
Whose graciousness and kindness
Is known by all
Lady who has never ceased in
Listening and learning
Who kept her heart open
And found a great wide world
Foundation of generations
Foundations of CoChee
Stand upon her work

(poem to my mother 2010)

January 2018

I am sitting in my husband's lap, sobbing uncontrollably, saying how much I miss her (my mom) I want to talk to her, and give her a hug, and call her on the phone. I tell Mark that I know I need to move forward, and find joy and happiness again. I just don't know how. The sadness and grief are uncontrollable He just holds me and lets me cry, again.

This is the time for me where the pain is unbearable, like a knife through my heart. I am a walking zombie; when I am not crying hysterically. no normal now and you will always miss her and to let myself feel the pain. This isn't what I wanted to hear. I scoured the internet and bookstores pain. I didn't find it. There were places where I read it is difficult for a daughter to laose her mother and that it changed them. I never wanted someone to tell me it will get better. That I was not destined to live my life in this agony forever. People who have suffered loss are better. Because, they know that everyone is different.

There is no prescription for grief. It does help to honestly talk about it. In my experience, those people are few and far between. The ones who do- you may count a true friend

Later that week, I start going through her journals, her bible and I remember all the cards and letters she sent me.

I begin to go through them, this is my journey.

Presents

Dear Tonja & Shelby,

Thank you for coming to my birthday dinner. I worry about you driving so far by yourself. Thank you for the beautiful towels. I am eager to get them washed and in the bathroom closet. Hope you can get Pap Jim to take Shelby to school, so you can go to D.C. with me. I'm really looking forward to it.

Love,
Mom
(2009)

It was only a week after she died, before Christmas. I am walking in Walmart getting groceries and some things for presents... I hadn't had much time to shop and needed a miscellany of things. I see a fuzzy blanket she would love and I go to pick the color out before I remember- I can't buy her a blanket. It brings me to tears. I stand in the back corner of the aisles, hoping no one sees me.

She is the first one I want to call.

She is the first one I want to buy a present for.

She is the first person I think of---

It is strange how your heart never forgets; even when your mind knows she is not here.

I ended up buying the blanket. I gave it to a charity for elderly people in my area who wouldn't otherwise have gotten a Christmas gift. Mom would love that.

Let Go and Let God

God bless you,

   May your day be blessed with happiness, joy and God's caring Love.

Ton,

   Let go and let God. He has you in the palm of his hands.

Love,
Mom

"Let go and Let God". How many times had she said this to me? Too many to count. She knew I worried, and contemplated and got in my head. Okay Mom, I hear you. I prayed this simple prayer: Lord, help me, let me let go and let you take care of this. It became my mantra.

Two days later, I started reading her Bible; passages she had highlighted or notes on. I came upon a slip of paper with her handwriting. It was a list of people to pray for. It was a list of our family 20+ with a blessing. The Lord bless you and keep you. The Lord lift his countenance upon you, and be gracious. The Lord be gracious unto you. It is from the Bible, Numbers 6:24-26. I had learned this as a song in college choir.

So, I started singing it and thinking of my family. Somehow, doing what she would have done, reading what she would have read brought me peace and it seemed like she was still here, still with me.

Christmas break was over and I went back to work. It did not go well. In the midst of middle schoolers getting ready for Christmas break, flu season and my mother dying, I had screwed up. Hard to imagine, insert eye roll. I was embarrassed and overwhelmed and still sad. I cried almost the whole day. I will say this for all of the crap we lay on middle school kids, they know when to be nice and when one school nurse has had all she can take. Thanks kiddos.

Imagine my awe when the next two cards I read are these…

Tonja,

Thinking of you this A.M and Praying things are going really well in your life, especially your new job. I am up at 4am washing, ironing, arranging my fall closet and trying to catch up on thank you and get well cards.

Hope to see you soon.

Love,
Mom
10/01

Ton,

Don't forget for one minute that you are special and the world needs you. "Perhaps you were born for such a time as this" Esther 4:14

Love,
Mom
2004

My mother in her grace and wisdom still knew just what to tell me. By God's grace I found what I needed in that time. She definitely was here. There was no way that this could have happened by accident. It was a new job, I had started in August at a new middle school. I did frequently wonder what the hell I was doing there. Despite the fact that in the back of my head I felt like I was supposed to be there. I had wanted to work with younger kids but God had put me here in the middle of an incessant pool of hormones and needs.

The Esther quote for emphasis put it all in order for The beautiful irony in these letters astounds me. I'm listening mama and on some level it is apparent you are still here still hoping the best for me. It takes me a few days to lick my wounds, pride and get over myself. I can hear her voice telling me that with my courage to continue I can do anything and her favorite scripture to quote to me: "For I am convinced, that neither death nor life, nor angels nor principalities, nor powers, nor things present nor things to come, nor height nor depth, nor any other created thing, shall be able to separate us from the love of God which is in Christ Jesus our Lord". Romans 8:38-39.

Maybe this verse includes a mother's love. It seems this way to me and I wrap her love around me like a blanket. I continue to move forward with work, with my life. I put one foot in front of the other. There are days that is all I can do. But, I begin to do more than just one task after another.

It is the cold and dark part of winter, which I never really love to begin with. This winter seems especially bleak. On my bad days, I am barely keeping it together. Crying on the way home from work and going through the motions at home. I am beginning to be able to smile and laugh, it is not an all consumable grief like it was. However, I am aware that I probably seem like a zombie to my family and friends. The lights are on but no one is home. I am so wrapped up in my own grief; it is hard for me to deal with anyone else's: my dad's, my sister's, my children's. The empty vessel cannot fill the glass. I read something on social media today about how trouble shows true character; the egg, the potato and coffee bean all change in boiling water, one becomes hard, one becomes soft, and one becomes a lovely drink. At the bottom it says: you either become bitter or better with hardship. Which one will it be? I want to be better, I definitely want to be better than this. Again, I am not my best self. This week one of my co-workers asks me if maybe I should go on an anti-depressant. I half laugh through my tears and tell her I am on an anti-depressant. What I want to scream is: my mom JUST died.

I should be allowed to miss her and cry. I sarcastically think to myself that the anger stage of grief is because of stupid people.

NEWSFLASH: grief and loss are not depression. It is an appropriate emotion to loss.

To My Beautiful Daughter

To my beautiful daughter, with love
You are such a beautiful person
And I hope nothing ever changes
Your inner beauty
As you keep growing
Remember always
To look at things the way you do now
With sensitivity
Honesty
Compassion
And a touch of innocence
As you keep growing
Remember that people and situations
may not always be
as they appear
but if you remain true to yourself
it will be all right
With your outlook, you will see
The good in everything
And this will reflect back to you
When I look ahead
I see happiness for you on every level
Because it is what every mother
Wishes for her daughter. I love you.
(poem by Susan Polis Schutz, given to me on my graduation from
college 1996)

Love,
Mom

If I remain true to myself. If I can look at things with honesty and compassion. If I can give myself compassion and honesty. Can I do that? Yes, I kind of suck right now. But, I'm never going to be better if I don't give myself some time. Compassion…. For others it is not usually difficult for me to do this. I expect things from myself that I would never expect from anyone I hang this card on my mirror so I can see it and read it every day. I can remember who I am and be that woman again.

Being honest; again, no one should be expected to get over a loved one's death in a week or two or six. The funeral, wake, visitation is not a grieving period. I would have been more comfortable with grief in Old Testament times, where I could tear my dress, and scream and sit in a pile of ashes for weeks, then watch over my mother's body in a tomb so that in a year I could bury her bones. It seems like GRIEF in our modern world is a dirty word. Death is not something to "get over". It's not a virus. It's a process. In this YOLO, Live your best life, social media world that we live in, where is grief, where is pain?

People aren't comfortable with grief, with death, with dying. Being a nurse a part of me knew this. I'd seen many families in denial, or refuse to see loved ones because they didn't want to deal with death. Dealing with it myself and looking back I have to give my husband props. He let me sit in grief, he sat with me in grief for months. He has never been a talker but his quiet strength saved me in so many ways.

There are people in my life that didn't want to be around me. Understandably so, I was kind of a pain in the ass. I was sad, I was tired, I looked like a mess and felt even worse. To the people who were around me during this time; thank you does not even begin to cover it. I'll say it anyway, thank you for loving me through my worst.

I know God is keeping you safe….
But I miss you anyhow!

My Kite
I spent a lifetime trying to get you off the ground.
I ran with you- until we were both out of breath.
When you crashed, I add a longer tail.
You hit a rooftop, I patched, comforted and adjusted.
Trying to teach (you), each step of the way.
I watched as you were lifted by the wind.
I assured you, someday you'll fly.
Finally
You're airborne, but need much more string.
As I let out each twist of the ball of twine,
I feel a sadness with the joy,
As my kite moves farther away.
I know it won't be long
Until that beautiful creature will snap the line that binds us,
And will soar as she was meant to SOAR.
Free and Alone.
My kite is free, but never alone
She'll always be tied to my heart.

Love,
Mom
(1992)

Mothering

I did know God was keeping Mom safe. If anyone were with Jesus it was her. She sang hymns the day before she died, I'll fly away, Lilly of the Valley and Standing on the Promises of God. She told us she was going home and that we would be behind her. But, I sure did miss her. As deaths go, it was a good one. She got to come home and be with her family, and friends. And, it felt like a celebration. There was food, and family and singing. And mom, telling us to love each other more, that she was going to see Jesus and would see us soon.

When people say life repeats itself, it isn't trite. It's real. My mom was free...free from pain and suffering, free from worry. Forever tied to my heart. In this time, I was grieving my mama and letting go of "my kite" my oldest daughter. It felt like all I knew was letting go. Knowing that mom had worked a lifetime trying to get me to fly and now I was letting Shelby go (albeit slowly) was bittersweet. I knew the chorus of mom and I my senior year and freshmen year in college. It wasn't easy. We found a way, with some fights, hurt feelings, and lots of love. It is never easy to let go, I was learning this lesson the hard way. I would have to find a new way to relate to Shelby to let out her kite string and let her fly. I would have to know that I was forever tethered to my daughter and my mother with love and memories.

I'm telling you this now, because it is one of those epic fights in motherhood. I drew my line in the sand. I stood my ground. I am not particularly proud of this moment; although, I am glad I didn't let it go. It was when mom was sick, in the hospital with influenza, pneumonia and renal failure. I was driving back and forth to the hospital 2 hours away, working and attempting to maintain our house. I was exhausted, and it had been an exceptionally painful day at work. I came home and took a nap. Shelby came home and wanted something. Honestly, I don't remember what she wanted. Just that she went on a tirade about how I was lazy and couldn't do this for

13

her. I lost it. I really lost it. I yelled back, she yelled back. She went to grab her keys to "go somewhere". I said no, because my lazy self helps pay for your car. I stood in the middle of the driveway with my best superwoman pose, daring her to move her car. Of course, she did. My 5'4" in heels body did not deter her will to leave. So, I did what any mom would do: I jumped on the hood of her car. We stared at each other through the windshield. I slowly shook my head no. And then we started laughing hysterically.

The moral of the story is this: my 17 year old daughter didn't leave the house that day and we laughed. Mom won that battle. The worst part was that she called me lazy. It bothered be to the core. I was trying so hard. I was hoping to be the kind of mother and daughter that could be there for everyone. Superwoman pose aside, I am human. I am very human. I decided at that point to let my family in on it: I needed help, I needed rest, and I needed them to understand.

Hi Tonja:

Just wanted to say thank you for the slippers and pajamas. I will truly enjoy them. I enjoyed my stay with Shelby. Wish I could do it more. Hope you are feeling better. Call me if I can be of any help.

Love,
Mom
(2004)

You try to raise a daughter to be an independent confident young woman, and what happens? You succeed beyond your wildest dreams.

Love,
Mom
(2008)

Tonja & Sarah:

Just a note to say how Proud and happy I am for you both. You are building some happy memories. I am so glad I got to share in some of your rewards. It was a real treat for me, Pam, and Phyllis. I know everyone worked really hard. Keep up the good work and fun. Love you both bunches.

Love,
Mom
(5/2017)

So much of my mothering is wound up in my own mother. She was eternally patient with me. She had a way of spinning the situation to her liking, but in a kind and gentle way. Mostly, she was love. If she could tell me she was proud of me, I must be doing something right. Not that I am living to her standard exactly, jumping on the hood of cars and whatnot.

It reminds me of Miranda Lambert's song, "My mama came from a softer generation when you get a grip and bite your lip just to save a little face". This ain't my mama's mothering. It's a little more honest and raw. But, I hope my girls see the love. I don't mind the honesty. I always thought that the perfect on the outside veneer was setting yourself up for failure. I remember my mom talking to me as an adult about fairy tales and that maybe she shouldn't have let me idealize them so much. Life isn't a fairy tale, and marriage isn't perfect, she said. Perhaps, Shrek should be our "love story". And, that is how I see parenting too. Children need to see the reality.

There are days I regret being so honest. There are days I regret working and that I didn't homeschool the girls. Then I remember that me being moderately sane is probably important too. My oldest daughter would tell me I was too kind to her, I built her up too much. That it's okay I am more open with her sister, because they need that reality.

Mom always said, she did the best she could at the time. If she had guilt, I never knew it. Somehow she had an endless supply of time for me and still managed to read and rest and wear red lipstick. Now, there's a lesson for our generation. Maybe, it is our modern lifestyle. Maybe, my girls are in more activities than I was. Maybe, she was better at managing her time. I'm still working on the mom guilt.

If I accomplish nothing else, I want my girls to know I love them and would walk through fire for them. They are amazing ladies and perhaps that is the best recipe for guilt; knowing they are truly amazing people.

Springtime

Hello,

Welcome to Spring. I am sure your roses are blooming. The one you planted me is doing beautifully. Thank you for taking care of Sarah's birthday gift. I hope she likes it and understands my getting the wrong date. I do wish her happy Birthday and I love her. Hope to see you soon. Love, Mom (2012) Hi Ton, Hope you enjoyed your time home as much as we enoyed having you. I'm still enoying your Roses and afraid the last ones may freeze, it has turned so cold. I'll pick them and bring them in if we have frost. Been very busy at work and home. Finally got some cleaning done here. I think I have more energy when its cold. I had better hope for more. Dad and I are taking the truck and trailer to Uncle Eugene's Friday and helping Dill haul their wood. Eugene isn't able to do anything and Dill is exhausted. Pray for us to have plenty of energy and good weather. I talked to Pam today. She's fine and eagerly awaiting the Eagles new date. Talked to Phyllis and girls last night. They are busy as usual. I baked banana bread and took them a loaf. It was good. I wish you had some I won employee of the month (gift certificate yesterday, $25 free groceries). Not bad, huh? Take care and keep in touch.
Our prayers and Good wishes,

Love,
Mom & Dad

It is was one of those beautiful spring mornings. Where the birds were singing and my flowers were starting to bloom. It was a day that I would have called mom. We would have talked about all the birds we had seen and how many flowers we had seen. Whether or not I had planted my garden. I'm looking out my kitchen window watching bluebirds feast beneath the oak we planted, years ago. They fly in and out-eating the acorns and carrying them to their nests. It would have been a moment I called my mom. I would tell her about the birds and we would have agreed that it was a good sign for spring. I tell her in my heart and smile at the pang that I won't hear her voice today. There are so many moments like this. Just last week, I wanted to call her when I harvested so many vegetables out of my garden: tomatoes, peppers, kohlrabi, and basil. We both love nature, birds and gardening. It was a love she nurtured early on. Then I reach out to call her and I realized I can't. Early on I would have cried. Now I go to a spot, my bedroom or outside on the porch and talk to her like I would have. It is a comfort to talk to her. I know now that there are other people who do this. So, it may sound insane but on some level they hear you, they know.

"The Profound One"

Her conception was profound. Her parents never expected to be bless by such joy in their later years. Her early childhood was marked by contentment with small things, tea parties, bike riding, roller skating. Climbing her favorite tree and singing with the birds, the beginning of her vocal training.

At 4 yrs. old her confidence had developed. She was comfortable being flower girl at her sisters wedding. The ring bearer wasn't so fortunate. She asked friends after the wedding, "Aren't you Proud of me?" She had performed well and was proud of it. At 8 during Sunday school, she reasoned that it is not wise to continually complain, because you will become like the boy who always cried "wolf". Noone will listen when the problem is real, "Profound", I nearly fell off my seat when she said this.

An easy child to raise, studious, knew by age 10 where her future will lie. In the medical field. First deep interest in genetics. Concerned by cloning and testing decided to go into nursing. A way to share and care for others.

Honest in all things. Always direct and open, she was labeled by our friends as the most emphatic child they had ever met. Even though, as teachers, they had worked with a variety. In her early teens, decided on her own to become a Christian, reasoning that even if there are no rewards in after life, the peace and love now will be worth the effort. At this time, discussing God with her father asked him, "What are you waiting for?" This proved to be the most motivating question he had ever heard. "Profound"

"A Mother's Reflection of a Profound Daughter"
(1999)

I promise my mom really wrote this about me. I came remarkably close to not including it. But, how could I not; it was her thoughts on raising me. I knew as an adult she was proud of me. She always told me I was an easy child to raise. I had no idea how much. I had no idea she loved my honesty so much. I had no idea my conversations astounded them or brought my Dad Jesus. Sometimes, I feel like I was a better person at 16 than 40 something. Maybe… we all are in some ways. But, here my mom is telling me how "profound" I am. That I should go forth and people should be proud of me. At least, she is, dad is. I still cry now as I read this. I don't know if she knew she was leaving her legacy to me in her poems and letter's; but, she did. Knowing my mother, she did know. She knew that I might feel broken and worn down and would need to remember to be proud of myself. There are days I have told my husband that I feel like I lost my biggest cheerleader. I didn't: she left pieces of herself here.

I just have to pick them up and remember.

"On Life's Thoroughfares, We meet with Angels Unaware"

I've never seen God, but I know how I feel
Its people like you, who make God "so real"
My God is no stranger, He's friendly and gay,
He doesn't ask me to weep when I pray.

It seems that I pass him often each day.
In faces of people I meet on my way.
He's the stars in Heaven, A smile on a face.
A leaf on a tree, A flower in a vase.
God is Winter, Autumn, Summer & Spring,

God is Every Real Wonderful Thing.
I wish I could meet him,
More than I do.
I would if there were "More people" like you.

I don't remember Mom every telling me why she wrote this or who it was to. Just that she sent it to me in one of her weekly letters. If anyone embodied God's loving kindness, it had to be my mother. We shared a love of nature and a philosophy, if you will, of God's divine in nature. We also frequently Shared poems with one another. Perhaps I miss her so much because of these things. I don't have another person in my life like her.

I think that I want More and more to be like her. To aspire to show the love she showed.

My Cheerleader

Love it here...
Miss you there!
But not much longer. Take care and keep in touch.
WE love you deeply and pray daily for your health, safety and
all your needs.

Love,
Mom & Dad
(1993)

It was my sophomore year in college and they were in Florida for the winter. I didn't realize how much I missed them until that winter. It was a long winter without being able to see them. It was my first glimpse of knowing what my life might be like without them. But, I had these weekly reminders of their love and prayers. I am sure she does love it there, in heaven. It makes me think that she is still praying for me and, that does give me comfort. My cheerleader is with me in a way.

Baking

Dear Ton,

Here is the recipe you asked for, hope you are having a good week. Tell the girls and Mark I love them. Banana Bread

1 ¾ cup All purpose flour
1 ¼ tsp baking powder bananas and milk and eggs. Slowly fold in dry
½ tsp baking soda Cream shortening and sugar, until light. Add ingredients, mix well.
Turn into slightly greased
¾ tsp salt loaf pan
1/3 cup shortening
1 cup mashed ripe bananas
2/3 cup sugar
2 eggs
2 TBSP milk

Cream shortening and sugar, until light. Add bananas and milk and eggs. Slowly fold in dry ingredients, mix well. Turn into slightly greased loaf pan. Bake at 350 for 30 minutes or until done. (2009)

My mom's banana bread was epic. She made it when my sister catered. She made it for all of us… family, friends. It was probably a few months After Mom died. I was cleaning out cabinets and found the "brownie plate". A simple plate with pink hearts and blue flowers that she gave filled Brownies. I would bring the plate back and she would fill it back up with banana bread, zucchini bread, lemon cake, cookies, brownies or whatever baked goods she was making at the time. She was forever baking and bringing things for her children or grandkids. It was one of her love languages, I think. She was a feeder. You never left her table or house hungry.

Tending the Garden

Tonja,

I picked another Rose today, as beautiful as the rest. There are more buds. I hope they don't get frozen. I look at the roses often and I remember the day you planted the bush and how much care you gave it all summer. It has paid off. I have enjoyed it greatly. Thanks a lot.

Our prayers and good wishes are with you

Love
Mom & Dad.

Hello Tonja,

Just need to say "Hello". Hope all is well and you will find time to stop in soon. It has been beautiful here. Your flowers are gorgeous. The roses are Blooming again. Six buds ready to pop. We are all enjoying them. I kept Cade today, after prayer breakfast. He is so big you won't believe him. He wears me out. Ashley has her hands full lifting him not, but it doesn't slow her down. Kara is performing at EC Halftime show Friday and parade Saturday. I hope to go to game Friday night.

Hope to see you soon.

Love,
Mom

It's another one of those days for me…. It is the beginning of October, 2 days past mom's birthday. The sun is shining, the birds are singing. I miss her. I would normally have picked out something Cozy or flowers (mums for her) and gone to see her. We'd have gone to lunch or library or gotten a pedicure. Thinking of her now, I realize how much, How often, How deeply I miss her. Even now as I read her card I get another message from her. How she remembered how I planted the rose bush Cared for it. How my attention and care made a difference. Would she know that years later I would need to hear those words again to find strength Continue to care for my patients and family. Legacies are a unique and strange thing I think. I got a catalog from world vision today and decided Would be my present to my mom this year. I'm buying chickens for a village in Southeast Asia; she would love that.

Dearest Tonja,

I am up early waiting for Alverta to pick up her church key. I cleaned the church for her last week and have her key. Sunrise is beautiful. Reminds me of a rise over the ocean. Your flowers are still more beautiful every day. The rose has 3 more buds and another one blooming. I cannot believe how much one bush can bloom. It has been a very busy week of work and taking care of Dad and Phyllis. She wasn't able to drive to the office Wednesday and Thursday. I drove And stayed with her. Karl has worked very little this week. He will miss it payday. The girls have had a good week in school. Kara went to game last night, with Christen and her Dad. Ash and Kyle stayed here and rode golf cart dark. I took them to get a movie and The B&G for a milk shake. They were excellent and had fun. The girls slept over. Rick and Phyllis went to the show in Indianapolis. The yard looks real good this week. Big John trimmed and mowed. He did a great job. Dad wasn't able to mow this week. Im getting ready for my Garage sale. A lot of work but worth the effort. I'm getting ready for Uncle Harold's party this evening. Baking, cooking & fretting. (Sat evening). All of the family was there except you, Karl and Kara Had to work. I had a good visit with Steph and Amy. They want to see you when you get home. We came home in time to pick up Karl from work, He is spending the night, has to be at work at 8 am tomorrow.

Hope all is well with you. I am sitting with my feet up now.

Much love and prayers,
Mom
(1996)

29

Hi Tonja,

Just a note to remind you, I love you, miss you and am praying for your health, adjustments and protection. My busy life has not slowed down. In addition to my regular schedule, I kept Cade Thursday after work and all day today (wed). He is a dream, so happy, and energetic. I really enjoy him. Phyllis is having a tough time leaving him. Ashley has soccer on Tuesday. Phyllis is worn out after working, little rest. Cade still doesn't sleep much at night. I took pictures of your Roses today and picked one. They are too beautiful not to look at all day. I to Sherman House Tuesday to make a firm commitment to the party room. The activity director is off on Tuesday. I have an appointment Monday. deposited $375 in your account. Let me know if you need more. "Remember dreams come true for those who work while they dream. Sweet dreams.

Love,
Mom
(1996)

Mom wrote these and many others my senior year in college. I was in Lexington. I would get the blow by blow of her day or weekend. She used to journal every day and occasionally I would look at it or she would share it with m. As a kid, I never understood it. It wasn't what I thought a journal should be. It certainly wasn't like my journal or like the journals that I had done in school. It was a laundry list of all the things she had done. Occasionally she would include a bible verse or antecdote that she had read somewhere. Not her feelings, not how her enormous amount of activity made her feel. I don't know if my Dad ever came home and said what did you do today? If he did I certainly never heard him ask her. I don't know if it is part Of her born in the depression, child during WW 2-- practicality. I don't know if she felt like she had to justify her day. I think maybe that is part of it. No, as an adult I get that. That somedays you need to feel like you accomplished something. To look at your busy day on paper and say okay, this is where my time went. I wish I would have asked her. I hope that she never felt like she had to justify herself. I hope she knew she was loved. I think so. I never felt like there was unfinished business between us.

God's Sense of Humor

Dear Ton,

I am getting ready for my garage sale for Dr. Dang's mission. Ashley is helping me organize everything. I'm hoping to get several hundred dollars to send to him. I went through some of your old dresses and just couldn't part with them. Hope to see you soon.

Love you and praying for you.

Love,
Mom

Dr. Dang is a missionary from, and at that time, based in Vietnam. Mom was incessantly collecting change that she often found in parking lots, and having sales, collecting others unused items and having a garage sale. The change she called her pennies from heaven.

Several months after she sent me this letter; mom showed me a letter Dr. Dang had sent her. They were both trying to unravel the mystery of where the monthly money that my mom had sent into the Mission office for Dr. Dang had gone to. Dr. Dang had not received monthly payments from my mother. She had worked so hard to see to it that he got his monthly support from her and my Dad. In it Dr. Dang quotes my mother, "Yes, God certainly does have a sense of humor and works everything out in his own due time." With mom's inquiry the mission office had found the account with mom's money earmarked for Dr. Dang. They were able to transfer the funds to Dr. Dang. In the account, was enough money to build a church in Cochee, Vietnam.

Unbeknownst to my mom, Dr Dang and his wife had fervently prayed for a church and the funds to build a church. Had he asked her to finance a church, she would have never believed she could do that herself.

But as my mom frequently said to me, "All things come together for those who follow Christ".

To me, this is an eternal lesson in life. Sometimes we are impatient, sometimes we don't understand. Sometimes we think our hard work is not paying off. We don't have the full story. God's vision has not yet come to fruition. You may have "small gifts" (pennies from heaven), but with God all things are possible. We just have to persevere and enjoy God's timing. And sometimes, His sense of humor.

"Leaving Time"

I'm always here...
Always as near as your need, always caring,
No matter what.
Dad and I are in earnest prayer for a good week for you. We know you will do your best and so will the Lord.

Love,
Mom

In her life, she was always there for me. I had often taken that presence for granted. That ever present concern and love. I do still hope that prayers continue on. That she prays for us in heaven.

There are days, I know she is. That I can sense her presence.

My mom is everywhere I go.

Everything I see.

In every victory and defeat.

I am comforted by her words, by her love.

In some way, she has been preparing me for life without her forever.

But, I guess, that is what good mothers do.

My mother is still sending me messages. Telling me what I need to hear. Reading the last book she read, which was not easy. She told me to read it that I would love it. There are so many layers and it is speaking to me.

It is about a scientist researching elephants. Not just elephants, but elephant grief. It is about the elephant herd caring for the young and each other. It is about a mother and daughter and their love for each other. Saying goodbye and hello again. If my mom could have written a novel for me at the end of her life this would have been it.

It is called "Leaving Time" by Jodi Piccoult. Leaving Time… At the end of the book there is a quote, "If you think about someone you have loved, they are with you." And, that is it, isn't it? If I am thinking about my mom, what she would have said, or told me then she is with me.

Amish Friendship Bread
Starter – (Do not refrigerate)
3 C milk 3 cups sugar 3 C flour

Day 1 Mix milk, Sugar + flour
Day 2 – 4 stir each day
Day 5 add 1C each milk, sugar, flour
Day 6 – 9 stir each day,
" 10 add 1C each milk, sugar, flour (over)

into 3 containers put 1 C mixture, share with friends. With remaining batter make bread. ⅔ C oil 2¼ C flour, 1 C. Sugar. 3 eggs 1½ tsp Soda, 1½ tsp Cinnamon 1½ tsp salt 1½ tsp B.P. add to starter. Pour into 2 loaf pans or 1 Bundt pan, greased & floured. Bake 350° 45 mins. you can add Raisins, Blueberries, Nuts, apples, bananas